Get Motoring!

Scooters

by Dalton Rains

FOCUS READERS

SCOUT

www.focusreaders.com

Focus Readers is distributed by North Star Editions:
sales@northstareditions.com | 888-417-0195

Produced for Focus Readers by Red Line Editorial.

Photographs ©: Shutterstock Images, cover, 1, 4, 7, 8–9, 11 (top), 11 (bottom), 13, 14–15, 16 (top left), 16 (top right), 16 (bottom left), 16 (bottom right)

Library of Congress Cataloging-in-Publication Data
Names: Rains, Dalton, author.
Title: Scooters / by Dalton Rains.
Description: Mendota Heights, MN : Focus Readers, [2024] | Series: Get motoring! | Includes index. | Audience: Grades K-1
Identifiers: LCCN 2023031684 (print) | LCCN 2023031685 (ebook) | ISBN 9798889980100 (hardcover) | ISBN 9798889980537 (paperback) | ISBN 9798889981381 (pdf) | ISBN 9798889980964 (ebook)
Subjects: LCSH: Scooters--Juvenile literature. | Scootering--Juvenile literature.
Classification: LCC TT174.5.S35 R35 2024 (print) | LCC TT174.5.S35 (ebook) | DDC 629.227/5--dc23/eng/20230801
LC record available at https://lccn.loc.gov/2023031684
LC ebook record available at https://lccn.loc.gov/2023031685

Printed in the United States of America
Mankato, MN
012024

About the Author

Dalton Rains is a writer and editor who lives in Minnesota.

Table of Contents

road

Scooters

Scooters drive on roads. They are small, but they can be very useful.

One or two people can
ride on a scooter.
Each rider wears a **helmet**.
Helmets help protect riders
if they fall.

helmet

Parts

A scooter has two small **wheels**.

The seat is above the back wheel.

The rider's feet go on the footrest.

seat
footrest
wheel

A scooter has a **headlight**.

It also has **handlebars**.

Riders use the handlebars

to steer.

Riders also use the handlebars

to go faster and stop.

headlight

handlebars

Uses

Scooters cannot go very fast.

But they are easy to ride.

They are also easy to park.

So, people often ride scooters

in cities.

Scooters help people travel short distances.

Older students may ride scooters to school.

Adults may ride scooters to work.

Glossary

handlebars

helmet

headlight

wheels

Index